Understanding Women

Unlock the mystery of women's mind and learn the languages of love to look more attractive and date the women you want

By Gary Wayne

© Copyright 2019 by Gary Wayne - All rights reserved.

This eBook is provided with the sole purpose of providing relevant information on a specific topic for which every reasonable effort has been made to ensure that it is both accurate and reasonable. Nevertheless, by purchasing this eBook you consent to the fact that the author, as well as the publisher, are in no way experts on the topics contained herein, regardless of any claims as such that may be made within. As such, any suggestions or recommendations that are made within are done so purely for entertainment value. This is a legally binding declaration that is considered both valid and fair by both the Committee of Publishers Association and the American Bar Association and should be considered as legally binding within the United States.

The reproduction, transmission, and duplication of any of the content found herein, including any specific or extended information will be done as an illegal act regardless of the end form the information ultimately takes. This includes copied versions of the work both physical, digital and audio unless express consent of the Publisher is provided beforehand. Any additional rights reserved.

Furthermore, the information that can be found within the pages described forthwith shall be considered both accurate and truthful when it comes to the recounting of facts. As such, any use, correct or incorrect, of the provided information will render the Publisher free of responsibility as to the actions taken outside of their direct purview. Regardless, there are zero scenarios where the original author or the Publisher can be deemed liable in any fashion for any damages or hardships that may result from any of the information discussed herein.

Additionally, the information in the following pages is intended only for informational purposes and should thus be thought of as universal. Trademarks that are mentioned are done without written consent and can in no way be considered an endorsement from the trademark holder.

INTRODUCTION

Men say that women are difficult to understand, so today, I am going to help them understand each other. So women, make sure your partner reads this.

Pay attention, men. One of the greatest needs that women have in love relationships is to feel protected. I do not mean we want a bodyguard; what a woman wants is to feel emotionally protected.

Many of the negative behaviors and attitudes that men repudiate in women are caused because they do not feel protected. For example, a woman does not feel safe when a man is irresponsible; criticism excludes her, judges her, does not communicate, or shows coldness. Given these behaviors, a woman becomes cold, grumpy, and sexually indifferent. Alternatively, you can also go to the opposite extreme and become a possessive, jealous, and sticky partner.

If any of these descriptions fit your wife, you may wonder, what can I do to make her feel protected?

Gentlemen, I stress the following: When a woman feels protected, she is more relaxed and confident. This means that you can do your best and become your ideal partner. Protect her, and you will become her superhero!

CHAPTER 1: HOW TO UNDERSTAND WOMEN

If you notice that you struggle to understand women in your life, do not worry; it is not as complicated as you imagine. The trick to understanding them is to avoid assumptions and know them individually. It could be an acquaintance, a relative or your partner; In any case, if you dedicate some time to talk and listen with sincerity, you will soon have a more precise notion of his person and his motivations. It may also be useful for you to know their problems and learn to recognize and question some common gender stereotypes.

Meet a person

Avoid making assumptions about her.

You will have a hard time understanding a person if you assume you know everything (or something in particular) about them. When you meet a woman, first forget all assumptions about what you think or feel. Do not conclude that you know something in particular about your life, your preferences, or your primary values.

For example, if she is single, do not assume she is lonely and seeks a relationship. Not all women are interested in having a romantic partner.

It can be difficult to recognize your assumptions. If you notice that you think something about a woman in your life, stop and ask yourself: "Why do I feel about that? Is there any reason why I think so about it?

Recognize that he has his own identity.

Remember that each woman is a unique and individual person, just like you. She has her own life story, circumstances, and experiences that have shaped the person she is. As you get to know her, try to consider her a person before paying attention to her sex or some preconceived notion of how "she" should be a woman.

This does not mean that you have to ignore their sex since this is an integral part of the identity of most people. Just recognize that it does not define your character entirely.

Ask him questions about his feelings, thoughts, and beliefs.

One of the most effective ways to meet and understand anyone is to talk to him. If you are interested in following a woman better, ask her questions. Just ensure that the questions are not very personal or invasive, especially if you do not know her very well. For example, you could ask questions like the following:

- "What do you like to do to have fun?"
- "What do you think of this problem?"
- "Why did you choose that profession?"
- "What are some of the goals you hope to achieve one day?"

Listen actively to everything you have to say.

Asking questions and engaging in conversation will only help you understand a woman, if you pay attention to what she says. When you speak, make an effort to listen to it and understand what it means. Do not dedicate the whole conversation to planning what you are going to say next. Better listen to it and then decide how to respond.

If you do not understand something, repeat it with your own words or ask him to clarify it.

For example, you could say, "It seems you don't want to vote for Johnson because you don't like his position around environmental issues, right?"

Pay attention to your body language.

Listening to a person's words is not the only way to understand them. It is also important that you pay attention to your nonverbal clues, such as your facial expressions and posture. When you spend time with a woman or talk with her, watch what her face and body do.

For example, if you make eye contact, smile, and leave your arms loose at your sides, you are likely to feel comfortable and relaxed.

If you look at the floor and cross your arms, you may feel nervous, shy, or worried.

Spend time with her socially, if possible.

Spending time near someone can help you understand this person better. If you can hang out socializing with her, you will have the opportunity to observe how she behaves in different situations and around different people. Depending on how well you know her and how comfortable she is with you, invite her to spend time with you alone or in a group.

Make your invitation specific. For example, instead of asking an ambiguous question like "Do you ever want to go out with me?", you might ask "I'll go to a night of general knowledge questions with some friends on Friday, would you like to go?"

For time alone, invite her to do something with little pressure that allows you to talk with her and get to know her a little. For example, you could invite her for coffee or lunch so they can chat.

Talk to other people who know her to get different perspectives.

If you have trouble understanding a person's behavior, it can sometimes be helpful to talk to friends or acquaintances. They could tell you the reasons why he behaves, thinks, or speaks as he does.

For example, you could say, "You've known Sarah for a long time. Why do you always bother when the issue of parrots arises?

Try to put yourself in their shoes.

Developing a solid notion of empathy is an important part of understanding everyone. Try to imagine yourself in their circumstances. Ask yourself what you would think and feel in the same situation.

For example, you might think of something like, "Monica seems very forgetful at times, but she works double shifts and takes care of a child at home. She is likely to be very overwhelmed and tired most of the time."

Find out about the unique problems that women face.

Even if you live in a society in which the sexes are considered equal on a legal and social level, men and women face their unique problems and challenges. To understand women, try to look at the big picture in general and understand what types of pressures and biases they face and what men do not experience.

For example, you could read articles, books, or opinion texts about problems such as differences in the treatment of men and women by the medical professional or the challenges faced by women in the workplace.

If a woman complains about the challenges and frustrations of being one, she resists the need to become defensive or dismiss her. Keep an open mind and try to see things from your perspective.

Be understanding of romantic relationships

Give your partner your full attention when they are together. Even if you have a close relationship with a woman, you will have difficulty understanding her entirely if you are not present and do not give her your attention. You do not have to concentrate on it all together 24 hours a day and seven days a week, but give it your attention when they have a good time together. Save your phone and other distractions, and listen carefully to what you have to say.

When they talk, try to understand what you say before responding. Ask questions after listening.

If he feels that you pay attention to him and strive to understand it, he will be more likely to do the same for you.

Take an active interest in the things that matter to you.

You will understand your partner better and take more advantage of their relationship if at least you feel a little interest in things that are important to her. Ask her what she likes to do, what her goals and dreams are, and what causes and beliefs are most important to her. Find ways to participate in some of your favorite hobbies.

This could be as simple as watching your favorite show with her or joining her sometimes when playing her favorite video game.

Ask questions about things that interest you. For example, ask, "What do you like most about this book?" or "How did you like rock climbing?"

Knowing what matters to you will not only bring you closer but also give you more information about your identity as a person.

Do not make accusations or draw hasty conclusions during discussions. If your partner does something that you do not understand or agree with, do not rush to complain or make accusations. This will make him defensive and have more difficulties to capture his perspective and solve the situation. Instead, communicate with her about what you feel and ask her calmly and respectfully to explain her behavior.

For example, you could say, "It hurts me a lot, and it confuses me that you have made this comment about my brother. Why did you say it?

Do not use language that generates accusations or assumptions. For example, do not say, "You always try to belittle my family and me so that you feel better about yourself!"

Ask him how he is doing.

If you do not know for sure how your partner feels or what he thinks, the best way to find out is to ask. Be sure to pay close attention to their answers, and ask me to clarify what you still do not understand.

You can ask open-ended questions, such as "How do you feel now?" or more specific ones, like "Are you upset about the discussion we had earlier?"

If he gives you an elusive response or says, he does not want to talk about it, do not push him or act resentfully. Instead, say something like, "Okay, I understand, but I'll be here if you want to talk."

Connect with your thoughts and feelings.
It might seem strange to you, but understanding you better can make you understand your partner more easily. If you do not know for sure what is going on in your mind and your heart, you will have more difficulty connecting with what you are thinking and feeling. Spend some time every day consciously paying attention to your own emotions, thoughts, and physical sensations.

Do not try to judge or analyze your thoughts and feelings. Just name them and give them a name. For example, you might think, "When I argue with Susan, I feel scared. I worry that I can lose it. My shoulders get tense, and my heart speeds up."

CHAPTER 2: THE GAME OF SEDUCTION: WHAT DOES PSYCHOLOGY SAY?

As if it were any other game, in seduction, we can improve a lot. Knowing the rules of the game and some tricks offered by Psychology can help us achieve it.

Seduction, contrary to what many people may believe, is not a concept attributable solely to the sexual or erotic realm. In our day-to-day life, there are often many situations in which we have to "seduce" in one way or another.

Do not we have to seduce who makes us a job interview? Alternatively, to those who come to witness an exhibition of ours? Tempt is to convince, to persuade a person or group of people to choose us in a particular context or choose an option that interests us.

The word 'seduction' comes from the Latin *seducere*, which combines the suffix is (separation) with the verb Dakar (guiding, or directing), and implies separating or leading someone out of their way or position. This is only the original meaning, but throughout history, it has been given different senses.

It is in the Bible, in its translation into Latin, that this verb happens to have a much more concrete connotation, reducing its meaning to the act of deception or the concealment of information to obtain some reward (when the snake seduces Eve in the garden of Eden).

However, this time, we will address the most popular and widespread meaning of seduction, which implies a suggestion or a conviction to get an erotic encounter or any erotic or emotional bonding.

Is seducing a game?

Yes, it is. Seduce is a very complex game, sometimes pleasant, sometimes fun, sometimes unfair, sometimes painful, sometimes frustrating ... But a game and the first thing that should be done is to try to understand it; its rules, its tricks, its risks, its limits, and its times.

If we have all that information, we will be able to decide whether to play or not, and we will be able to know how to play if we choose to play seduction. If it is agreed to play seduction it is because every aspect of the game has been taken into account, and, on the scale, it has weighed more pleasure or satisfaction than pain or suffering.

Seducing is not a zero-sum game in which if you "win," the other person "loses." Instead, it could be included in cooperative games: those in which the participants do not compete, but seek mutual benefit. In fact, rather than being a cooperative game per se, if in the process of seducing the game, it becomes cooperative, it will be a definite sign that you are playing well.

In the same way that it is about framing seduction within the game theory, it is also necessary to separate it from some myths that surround it. Seduction is not mathematical; it is not exact or excessively predictable.

Films like "Hitch" (2005) have reinforced ideas such as the guru who gives "infallible" advice about how to tie or seduce, regardless of anything else. This idea is very far from reality because there are so many variables that come into play when it comes to seducing that it is impossible to control them all.

What psychological variables influence seduction?

Psychology goes to our rescue to better understand seduction. This discipline, through the scientific study of human behavior, introduces us to what variables are decisive in the game, so that we can give our best version.

These variables are far from being advice, guidelines, or instructions that work universally in any context and with any person, but rather describe what should be taken into account when participating in this game.

Self-knowledge and acceptance

To the extent that we know each other at all levels, we can set the limits that have to do with what we like and do not like, as well as knowing how far we can get in the game.

Some contexts favor us more and settings in which we cannot show our best version. Accepting yourself as one or one is an exercise much more complicated than it may seem beforehand; it seems inevitable to be able to play the best cards when it comes to seducing.

Expectations

It is one of the variables that can cause more discomfort because it is a source of misunderstanding and confusion when it is not taken into account. Setting realistic expectations is a way to prevent awkward situations and avoid suffering.

In the same way that expectations that are too high concerning having a relationship with someone can frustrate us - if this relationship is not finally given - setting expectations that are too low will prevent us from having a relaxed and safe attitude.

- **Attention**

Entering the basic psychological processes, the focus is the process that allows us to discriminate between what is important and what is not, which makes it the main variable when it comes to seducing.

The attention will allow us to focus our cognitive resources on actions such as focusing on the communication of the person with whom we play to seduce, in their physical traits, in their way of dressing, in their style, in the other people who are in our around and in all context keys that give us some information that we consider relevant, prioritizing them over different types of stimuli.

- **Perception**

It is the ability we have to obtain direct information about the environment through our senses. Although attention allows us to focus and discriminate between stimuli, the perception will enable us to process, interpret them, and thus choose the best option to interact.

In seduction, only what we perceive is not an option. We must give meaning to the verbal cues that are provided to us, to non-verbal communication, and even to sets of stimuli as, in principle, unimportant, such as smells, as there is more and more literature about them, especially pheromones.

- **Memory**

It is not only essential to obtain information from our partner or playmate, but also retain that information: work with it. The ways to keep information give rise to the two main types of memory:

  - The short-term memory is the one that could help us in maintaining information that will no longer be available shortly after being received - unless we make an effort to the contrary or have elements that make it very easy to encode - like a phone number or an address.
  - The long-term memory , which can be used to retain the information of the day in which you have interacted with a person, making that information available to a possible second appointment or meeting, and through the retrieval of information on biographical facts, to make them available for a

conversation; for example, to be able to talk about the first concert we have gone to in a discussion about tastes and musical experiences.

- **Motivation**

It has to do with the amount of resources we are willing to use to obtain a concrete result. That is, motivation represents the degree of interest in doing something.

In seduction, it is convenient to do a small introspection exercise to know how motivated and motivated we are with the game, and make sure that we are playing to seduce with the person we want and the way we want and not because there is another type of motivation different from what has to do with the game itself. There are two types of motivations:

- Extrinsic motivation, which represents the interest in achieving a goal, regardless of the process until it is achieved (the process until obtaining the driver's license, or studying with the sole intention of getting a degree that we need).
- Intrinsic motivation, which is one that represents the interest in the process itself until reaching the goal rather than the goal itself (learn to cook or read a book). In the game of seduction, it is recommended to have an intrinsic motivation, oriented in the process, in the game itself, rather than the goal or the result.

- **Emotion**

And how emotions weren't going to be present! It is the essence of the game that makes us excited. In the beginning, it was commented that we will not always be happy to play seduce, but there is no doubt that it will still excite us, and if it is not, maybe I do not know your game.

Moreover, in this hypothetical balance in which the advantages of playing weigh more than the inconveniences, emotions have to be present, to a greater or lesser extent if the game excites us or should not have much weight when deciding whether to seduce or not at a particular time.

Sexual or erotic desire and seduction

Sexual or erotic desire, a very complex concept, hardly describable and with a very high motivational power, is closely related to seduction. Surely, it makes little sense to try to seduce someone we do not want erotically. Desire is also a variable to consider in seduction. Specifically, it is a sexual variable that can determine the way we play in the following ways:

Desire Direction

When we seduce, we seek a concrete goal. On the erotic level, there are two types of directions that have to do with the target, with the realization of our desires and with its nature.

In this way, we can talk about the " desire of the one ", which represents the desire for a specific person, without delving deeply into what is done in an intimate relationship (when we want someone, and we do not care much if we do something or another with that someone in a future relationship), and on the other hand, the " desire for what ", refers more to the desire to perform a particular type of erotic activity, weighing more power to carry it out than the one with whom to do it. To seduce, we have to adapt the way we play to our direction of erotic desire.

Roles of desire in seduction

It refers to the way we play, to what behavioral mechanisms we activate to seduce that person we want. These roles are determined, above all, by our personality traits. In this way, there are two trends in this regard:

- The elastic, which is defined as the role of "desiring" in which the person stands as active and takes the initiative (to carry out the first approach, to adopt an enthusiastic attitude, communicate more directly, praise and flatter ...).
- The *eromenia*, which is defined as the role of "desired," in which the person seduces from an attitude of being desired and, above all, of feeling desired.

Is seduction a matter of gender?

Gender is a social construction and influences seduction. It is difficult for a boy and a girl of the same age, with the same academic background, similar personality traits, and in the same location, to have a similar seduction history.

This is explained because in the game of seduction, today, there is a clear reflection of machismo, and that is that socially, the game of seduction is still much more penalized if it is carried out by a woman than by a man. This situation yet feeds the fear that a girl dares to seduce in the way she thinks is appropriate, especially if she is active when it comes to seducing or adopting a more energetic role.

Within our closest environment, the ideal would be that we fight to defeat the old stigmas about seduction if it is a woman who carries it out, to equate both situations and that both men and women can play this same game. , only with the same rules.

CHAPTER 3: HOW TO FLIRT WITHOUT BOTHERING WOMEN

You may use a phrase or a technique that a colleague has just discovered, but no matter how well you are, there is something that does not quite fit. We explain why.

Creepy' is one of the most difficult words to translate from English to any language. It is usually translated by 'creepy,' 'chungo' or 'grimous,' but none fits perfectly. There is, therefore, no equivalent that conveys that mutual feeling of fear, disgust, and discomfort that women feel when dealing with slugs and strangers in everyday situations.

Every night, in hundreds of bars and clubs, some men find the courage to try to establish a relationship with the female gender. They may use a phrase or a technique that a colleague has just discovered. However, sometimes, however noble their endeavors are, there is something that does not quite fit, and most likely, the girl in question will later say to her friends: "What a 'creepy'!". It has an explanation.

A man looking for a new romance is in the delicate balance of expressing interest to a woman without crossing the line.

Psychologists have been investigating in the swampy terrain of the uncomfortable and 'creepy' for years. Frank T. McAndrew, a professor at Knox College, published an empirical study about it last year. After hundreds of conversations and surveys with people of different gender, country, and social status, and collate their investigations with those of the Canadian psychologist Margo Watt, he ratified what we already suspected: in effect, the consensus represents men as more "creepy". They are, therefore, considered as a potential threat more than a potential female counterpart.

However, from very early in his research, it became clear that for women, this feeling has a lot to do with sex. The respondents spoke almost unanimously of the impression that the man who approached them did so for some sexual interest, which was not interpreted as harmless or flattering. McAndrew blames him for the fact that the potential risk of sexual abuse forces them to be especially alert. It is something that they have developed for "solid evolutionary reasons," says the psychologist, and, therefore, they are likely to distrust that man they face not only because it makes them feel uncomfortable, but also because they could be a pervert.

The old green myth exists

Men are generally aware of how easy it can be to get into such a misunderstanding. "Most women who are at a party or in a bar full of singles are usually interested in meeting funny and interesting men, but for their own sake, they start up their detectors, their natural defenses. This gives rise to one of the ironies of life: many men are afraid of being perceived as 'creepy,' which creates an added difficulty to their relationships. Consequently, a man looking for a new romance is in a delicate balancing act of expressing interest to a woman without crossing the line, "says the psychologist.

However, handsome men with labia tend to have less awkward encounters than physically ungrateful men. Other variables, such as age and racial prejudice, can also play an important role. "The myth of the old green exists for something," says McAndrew. "It's no secret that as men get older, they tend to retain an attraction to younger women, but when the time comes to the age difference becomes so great that the romantic approach changes worse," he explains.

The founder of the OkCupid dating website, Christian Rudder, has developed a standard rule: a person should not date someone who was half their age plus seven years. The norm can be fantastic if we think that, for example, someone of 38 would be too old for a person of 23, while someone of 50 would be able to date a partner of 86. However, the data of the pairings through the web confirm the pattern.

The deepest fear of men is that she humiliates him sexually, while women's one is that they might be injured.

One of the most popular "love advice" blogs in the US says that all men go through a 'creepy' phase in which they learn the ABC of romantic life. During this period, men are young and inexperienced, nervous and clumsy, and do not know how to read the signals that women send them. In other words, a learning stage is needed as a trial and error so that a man knows if a woman is interested in him or not.

Experts recommend

However, some believe that fear does not end up disappearing. "The deepest fear of women when interacting with a man is that they are going to hurt them, while that of the man is that she humiliates him sexually. Understanding this can help you relate to the opposite gender," say evolutionary psychologists Tucker Max and Geoffrey Miller in ' The Mating Grounds.' That is, if you are a man, make sure that the woman you are talking to feels safe. In addition, they recommend:

- Do not go to have sex. Go out to meet new people and have fun. It is a subtle change, but that way, you seem to be less desperate and anxious, and it will make you more fun and attractive to the rest.
- If you are looking at a woman's body and she catches you, keep eye contact and try to respond with a genuine smile. Do not look away, as the brain encodes it as a predatory reaction.
- In that same situation, you can also say something like: "You caught me looking at you. I am sorry, but I love that shirt. " Although she knows that you were looking at her, do not compliment her body but something about which she has made a decision (like her clothes) with which you will not be objectifying her and thus demonstrate social intelligence.
- It is difficult for a woman to reject a man openly, but they will do so if all their interaction with her revolves around sex. If you frame the relationship in terms of having a good time and meeting new people, anything

could happen. She will decide later if she feels attracted to you.
- There are three critical things in a conversation with a woman: 1) make sure she feels safe, 2) that she feels socially protected, and 3) don't neglect the attractiveness or your skills during the conversation.

10 Tactics (Infallible) To Be Attractive To A Woman

Be nice, be nice, behave yourself and keep yourself looking good. Easy, right? It is not complicated to imagine what may interest a woman in a man, even if each one of them is a different world. Or, more than a world, a universe. You know, a fun, friendly, entertaining, or affectionate personality is essential - especially in the long term - but it's not everything. What we often do not remember is how our perception, our genetics, and our most primary instincts interfere in the way of our relationships, in many cases, to facilitate them in a way that previously we could not have suspected, in other cases, to hinder them without know why.

Women may like anything (there is the example of Carla Bruni and Nicolas Sarkozy to corroborate it), but science, in its unstoppable social work, has wanted to guide the male gender on what it should do or how it should behave to attract the females to their love networks.

- **Enjoy yourself.** When a young man enters a position of responsibility above what his real age would expect, it is quite common to grow a thick beard. The reason that facial hair makes men appear older, more respectable, more aggressive, and indicates that their social status is more significant. The negative counterpart? That men with beards are less attractive to women (unless what they are looking for is an interesting mature, of course). It is the conclusion reached by an investigation by Barnaby J. Dickson and Paul L. Vasey, which indicated that the beard ages, in exchange for being a sign of social distinction. The reason is probably evolutionary since, as the anthropologists who conducted the study point out, the appearance (or conservation) of the beard in humans could have been due to a form of intragroup natural selection.

Calm down and count to three, you will be more attractive –Make sure you have a proper face: Do not confuse with a pretty face that, everything is said, also helps. A study by scientists at the University of Abertay Dundee in Scotland concluded that women, which puts them, is an excellent immune system. Fhionna Moore, the author of the study, said that "the more antibodies a man produces in response to a vaccine, the more attractive his face is." It is testosterone that matters at this point: the higher its levels, the stronger the immune system and, therefore, the more beautiful the face will be, the researcher said. Also, and as we will see later, men with more testosterone had lower levels of stress, a key factor.

- **Show yourself vulnerable.** The most current studies have shown that, perhaps, what some women want is not a man to guide and protect them, but quite the opposite: a couple they can easily manipulate. This is what the recent study by the

University of Tennessee-Knoxville pointed out, in which it was pointed out that biology had less and less weight in the decisions taken by women and, therefore, began to prefer other types of men, less physically active. The reason? "That men who were unable to compete with their peers physically focused on providing food to their spouses to buy their affection."

-Behave yourself badly. Although it seems contradictory to the previous point, there are still studies that support the popularly shared idea that women prefer "bastards." This is the case of an investigation presented this year at the University of San Antonio, in which the author, Kristina Durante, pointed out that not only women prefer handsome men and little scoundrels for a short-term relationship, but also to maintain a long relationship with them. Specifically, the teacher (marketing!) Found out those women who were spending their fertile week found sexy, handsome and rebellious men as the most attractive, a sign that they were the right candidates to be good parents. The important thing, after all, is not to be unnoticed.

The most virile attributes were preferred in the least technologically developed countries - Do not stress. Calm down and move on: you will be more attractive. The reasons why women prefer relaxed men do address not only the emotional (who would want to spend a lot of time next to a person who only hurries and insecurity transmits?) but also the physical. The stress hormone, cortisol, is the cause of men looking less attractive to women since, according to the study cited above and conducted at the University of Alberta, women preferred those men with a lower level of cortisol, which would be related to a better genetic configuration. Something that was accentuated during the fertile phase of the menstrual period. Showing less stress also means that we are better able to deal with complicated situations.

–Evolve. Is it true what is usually said about women preferring men who are strong, brave, and brave, in short, the profile of the prehistoric hunter, willing to bring dinner home every night? It seems that this is not really the case, but what women are pursuing (from an evolutionary point of view) is a man who can provide the necessary material resources, but which does not necessarily imply the unredeemed alpha male. In reality, a couple is pursued that is capable of adapting to the society in which they live: in ours, physical strength would no longer be as important as social skills, adaptive intelligence, or professional skills. This is what a study by Welsh doctor Robert Brooks affirmed, which pointed out that more virile attributes were preferred in less technologically developed countries.

- Ride her on a roller coaster. A good meal is not the best aphrodisiac; it seems to be, but to live a fast-paced situation that triggers the adrenaline of women. At least, this is what a study published this year at the University of British Columbia affirms. What the researchers discovered is that single people who had just come down from a theme park attraction considered people of the opposite sex who had accompanied them during the trip as much more attractive than before. However, the same was not the case with already engaged couples who had boarded the ride, a sign that taking a couple of turns on the roller coaster can seriously affect our judgment.

Eating vegetables embellishes skin pigmentation – Don't be happy. Not everything was going to be bad news: if you feel intensely dissatisfied with your life and let this be reflected in your natural expressions, it will be easier to seduce a woman. According to a study called Happy Boys, they end later: the impact of facial expressions on sexual attraction, while men prefer more fun women, the female gender tends to be more attracted to circumspect and melancholic men.. Not because of his personality itself, but because these were the most attractive facial expressions for women. Both for some and others, the manifestations of shame and sorrow on their faces were equally desirable sexually.

–Care your skin (and eat vegetables). Although few men, except David Beckham, would be able to admit in public that they like to take care of their body with creams and other ointments of ominous name, the truth is that doing so can be profitable in the relationship with women. These prefer bright and healthy, tanned skins, over pale and whitish, a characteristic that puts them before others, such as the masculinity of the faces or the musculature of their potential partners. Specifically, it was the golden touch of the faces that made them irresistible, according to a study by Ian Stephen, who discovered that it was the decisive factor in the responses of his respondents. "The healthy color of our faces is determined by the antioxidant carotenoid pigments we get from the fruit and vegetables of our diet," said Professor at University College London. Eat more vegetables, man.

–Make sure you have big eyes, prominent cheekbones, and a big chin. Unless the genetic inheritance has provided us with these physical attributes, it is complicated that we can naturally change them, except in case of divine intervention or after going through an expensive and little recommended facial surgery. These are the three physical characteristics that were most desirable by women, according to a study published by the Journal of Personality and Social Psychology. In it, the authors (two women and one man) pointed out that these three elements were essential for the female sex because their development is related to sexual maturity (case of the prominent chin), but they also appeal to the feelings of protection of the woman (what happened with big eyes). But, eye, they only worked if they went together. Those men who can combine the three characteristics will be the kings of the mambo.

CHAPTER 4: HOW TO CONQUER AN UNKNOWN WOMAN

Perhaps you have fallen in love with a girl you have seen on the bus, in the library, at school, in a disco, etc., and do not know how to start talking to him so that he shows interest in you and you can conquer it little by little.

In this chapter, we will show you how to seduce a woman you have never seen before and that you are hungry because she is your girl. Be very careful how you will talk to him initially because there are many men who, at the time they have the opportunity to start a conversation with that unknown woman who does not have the slightest idea that they will tell that girl.

It is precisely that kind of people who are always looking for exact phrases with which they can conquer the girl he likes, however, when it comes to having the girl in front of him, the phrases never come out as expected, and all the tactics of seduction end up being a failure.

Logically, all this happens because the most important from the beginning is the way you express yourself, the security you show, and the exciting thing that you may think of the girl. The attitude you take when seducing an unknown woman will be essential to conquer it.

The initial point to everything is to know how to talk to him and with what attitude you will approach him. If you know how to start a good conversation, without a doubt, the girl will allow you to continue with the conquest and in the same way if you do not know how to do it you will be condemned to a total rejection, and you will not even be able to dream of having something with that woman. So be very careful with what you are going to say and how you are going to behave when you first approach a girl you do not know.

How to flirt with an unknown woman?

You should keep in mind that it is not the same as trying to link a girl you have known for a long time than a woman who is unknown to you. And, to achieve an excellent initial impression, you must use several steps to understand how to seduce a woman you do not know. It is evident that the level of trust between her and you do not exist, so you must start to earn her trust and appreciation so that something can happen after flirting.

Three steps to flirt with an unknown woman

1st step:

If you see that it is inaccessible or next to him is a boy, do not try to seduce her because it is most likely that he is in love. On the contrary, if he does not stop looking at you, he plays with his lips and hair; it is a clear sign that he is very interested in you. In this case, come closer and greet her kindly.

2nd step:

When you approach her, notice if she has a boyfriend nearby not to make the initial mistake. For example, a ring, a pendant, some earrings, or any detail that refers to another person. Ask secretly if your lover or boyfriend gives these earrings. If the answer is definite, then forget to have any possibility; on the contrary, if the answer is negative will have to follow the next step.

3rd step:

If the answer is that he has no crush, then give him your phone number to call you if he has any interest in going out to dinner or dancing with you. If she shows you any excuse not to leave, then discard that possibility because she will never be interested. But if you accept flirting and the invitation to remember that you must take care of all the necessary details to make it a first date where she can become your girl.

The dream date and the words you should use

Remember that if you did not do the previous steps, try it because you may be rejected immediately because of your inexperience. If you never fall in love with a woman, and you feel very nervous, think positively, and that the woman agreed to go out with you because she likes you in a certain way and has corresponded to the flirtation that you have shown her, on the contrary, she would have rejected you from the beginning.

The words you say and your mood

The important thing at all times is how you feel internally because if you are happy, confident, and you feel great, you can say anything that comes to mind and seduce that girl. On the contrary, if you are a conformist, you have a bad mood, you hate life, you are shy or nervous, and then the woman you go out with will give little importance because the girls quickly detect the personality of each boy by merely presenting it. Your distrust will be your worst mistake. Even if you start a conversation with that girl, you may go blank and get even more nervous. Try to relax.

If the girl now ignores you

If the girl who initially responded to the flirting and accepted an exit now overlooks you, don't worry, it may be part of her mood. The important thing will be that these types of actions do not affect your morale. Thank him for agreeing to go out with you and say goodbye, he is not the only girl in the world, and you don't have to endure rudeness.

If she tells you to leave, then do not waste your time talking to that girl, and even if you like it a lot, you have a blur and a new account, turn to the other side and start another conversation; you don't have to endure her foolishness.

Maybe during that search, you find another nice girl, and with whom you can find a possibility, then why stagnate with that same woman. Time is money. If you let more than five minutes pass because of the bad comments of that first girl, you will be wasting your time. Now relax and start the entire process with peace of mind.

If you are very shy or nervous

You should try this whole process systematically. From how you greet people, ask for the time, address of a street, talk to the vendors of a shopping center, and get involved in job interviews, and so on. All this can help you lose your fear and gain more confidence.

Be very original when conversing

Try not to interact with her through the common questions like "How are you?", "What is your name?", "What are you doing?", "Are you single?" and so on. These questions can be so common that all you will get is that she will never look at you. Those questions are so dull that you will achieve accurately that, ultimately, bore that girl and lose the opportunity she had to realize something beautiful.

Try using other strategies such as making her laugh with any of your jokes; this is a useful seduction tactic. Remember that the idea is to break the ice as it gives rise, and you can do it in many ways. You must combine a bit of confusion and interest in it to have more than half the way secured. With this strategy, you will know what attitude he has and his real personality. Gradually, the trust between you and her will grow, and you can form something closer.

CHAPTER 5: HOW TO MAKE A GIRL HAVE SEX WITH YOU

Making a woman have sex with you is a dream come true. Having sex with a gorgeous woman is for everyone!

You may be looking for women for a formal relationship, or you may want to date her informally because you only find her sexually attractive.

First, the best way to have sex with a woman is to go out with her and take things that way.

You will fall in love with a great woman and have fun every step of the way.

However, whether you are dating a woman or sharing a sexually exciting friendship, making a move to have sex is complicated.

You cannot talk about it very soon.

Nor can you make a move to have sex with her unless she reciprocally approves your steps.

One of the biggest problems in making a girl have sex with you for the first time is the caution that is associated with it.

A wrong move and you can create an enormous division in the relationship.

Use these ten steps to make a girl have sex with you, and you really will not have problems to excite her or have sex with her.

However, if she doubts at any point, go back and apologize for going so fast. You may not have timed your moves correctly.

Make these ten moves well, and she will be more than happy to have sex with you. Discover in 10 steps how to warm a woman.

1. Let him see your excellent side. If you want to have sex with a woman, you have to be good enough to get her attention.

If she thinks you are desirable and everything she wants in a man, then half the work is done.

2. Let her know that you are interested in her. Talk to her, spend time with her and let her catch you looking at her discreetly every so often.

Ask him if you are interested without revealing too much!

If you ask her out without making her like it first, she will lose the excitement of the mysterious relationship. Make her wonder what you have in mind, and you will make her fall in love with you without asking her out.

3. Leave the Friend Zone. Unless you go out with her, the friend's zone is a scary place. Friends do not have sex with each other, and they avoid feeling sexually attracted to each other.

Be her friend, but not just another friend who has no sexual interest in her. Make it clear that you find her attractive and sexy.

Flirt sexually with her, flatter her clothes with sexual praise and talk to her dirty.

Both may be friends, but make her feel the sexual tension when you are close to her.

4. Spend more time with her. If you want to have sex with a girl, the only time you can use your magic is to have time alone with her.

You need to flirt sexually and make her feel comfortable with you. But you can't do that if there are other friends nearby.

Behave normally if there are other friends with her, but in the second in which they leave, say something like "finally ... now I can spend time alone with this sexy girl ..." or something similar that makes it clear that you find her attractive in A way more-than-friends.

5. Go out with her. You don't have to be an appointment to go out with her. Invite her to lunch together at work or do some diligence with her. By doing that, you are already taking the place of boyfriend in your mind. But always remember to keep the sexual emotion at the top. Or she will only see you as a friend.

6. Touch it and excite it. Touch is a powerful way to send the right signals without looking desperate. Find ways to touch your arm or take your hand promptly.

The more you touch her delicately and sensually, the more sexually excited she will be.

7. Invite her to your home. Invite her to your house or try to invite her to his house. You have already generated sexual tension. She knows you are not just a friend, and she knows you are attracted to her.

By getting comfortable in each other's homes, it will take you one-step closer to your room and your pants.

After all, if you are going to have sex with a woman soon, you need to make her feel comfortable in private spaces.

8. Give him some clues. Therefore, she thinks you are a good guy who is attracted to her. Anyway, that is not enough. You need to turn her on and force her to look at your sexy side.

Look elsewhere and stretch casually when you have an erection in your pants.

Let her see your abs and your underwear when you change your clothes at home. Always look the other way when you show your body to her.

It gives her enough time to admire you sexually without fear of being caught.

These involuntary movements will make her feel sexually attracted to you and want you.

9. Watch a movie together. Go on a date or stay at home and watch a movie. A movie involves a couple of hours of quiet time where they both feel very close.

It is here that you can lightly touch it with your arm or foot. Do it correctly and be patient, chemistry can be electrifying.

If you want to seduce a girl, unconsciously touch her arm with yours lightly while you are next to her. That will excite her in a short time!

10. Excite it correctly. If you want to know how to make a girl have sex with you, you need to remember that the whole focus is on sexually arousing her to kiss you.

Never try to force it, instead, be safe and slow before going fast.

CHAPTER 6: HOW TO BREAK THE BARRIER OF FRIENDS - HAVE YOUR FRIEND BECOME YOUR GIRLFRIEND.

Are you tired of being stuck in the friend zone? It is very frustrating when a woman, to whom you are very attracted, thinks of you as a brother. If you want to escape from the friend zone, I have good news; there is a way out.

1 - Change your style.

Most men do not understand the power of clothing in the field of attraction. You can increase your social value; make everyone trust you and your decisions just by creating a personal image that is comfortable, fresh, and striking.

Be sure to show the girl of your dreams the best version of yourself at all times. She has to discover that a man is hiding behind her friend's facade.

In addition, there is something else, imagine your reaction when women start flirting with you in the street. As a rule, women will be attracted to you if other women are also attracted to you.

2 - Use your absence to increase attraction.

We have to allow women to miss each other. Avoid looking like a desperate man; showing yourself in need will ultimately kill the attraction.

If you have plans, do not cancel them just because she called you at the last minute. If she thinks you are always available, your value as a man will disappear automatically.

Your time is a valuable and limited resource; make her strive to give him some of it.

Men with adventurous and exciting lives are magnets of women. You need to have a life of your own before any girl can be part of it.

3 - The only constant in life is change.

Women are attracted to interesting men and arouse their curiosity. If she thinks she has discovered everything you have to offer, the attraction will disappear.

You have to keep it thinking. Send mixed signals all the time.

For example, you can use your body language to send positive and negative signals. This creates tension and will keep her thinking about you.

Unless you can create tension between a girl and you, you will never be able to escape from the friend zone.

One last reflection

If you want to be in a relationship with a girl, you have to be willing to lose her. Otherwise, it will be tough to maintain control.

Women always test your ability to maintain control. They will try to take away that power, and if you allow it, you will lose the battle.

Many men think that if they please women, they will earn some points and reach their hearts. That is a lie. Remember that if you lose control, you will also lose the girl.

5 Ways to Get Out of the "Friends Zone"

Are you tired of being the "good guy " that women always trust but never fix, flirt, or sleep with?

Have you been waiting for the perfect time to get out of the "Friends Zone"?

Dr. Jeremy Nicholson, who calls himself the "doctor of attraction, " says the friend zone is the area in which a girl wants to have you in her life, but only at the platonic level.

It is a very frustrating area.

So how to get out of it?

Try any of these five ways to go from being the friend to being your beloved boyfriend.

The details:

1. Renegotiate the terms. If you want to leave the "Friends Zone," you need to renegotiate the terms of the relationship. When you take a friendship to a new level, you are not extending the friendship; you are creating a new relationship. Therefore, you should be able to negotiate the terms of the new relationship. Have you ever thought about merely asking him to change the status of your relationship? Try it; It may be exactly what she has been waiting for.

2. Stop looking so interested. This is scientifically known as the "Principle of Less Interest," as published by the authors Waller and Hill in 1951. When you value a person more than they value you, the relationship is already unbalanced. Try using the principle of least interest to regain your power. Looking less interested and being less available to her will make you look more valuable in her eyes, or at least reveal to her how much it depends on you.

3. Make you something "hard to get." It is the simple concept of supply and demand. People do not want what is right in front of them as much as they want what is difficult to achieve. Cialdini, the author of "Influence: Science and Practice," suggested that the easiest way to influence someone was to use the "shortage" principle. It is the same concept that your parents used to use when you took away your favorite toys because you misbehaved; once the toy was not within your reach, you wanted it more than anything, even though you weren't even playing with it at that time. Become difficult to reach her eyes, and you will become a person of more value to her.

4. Create some competition. It is important to be challenging to reach and seem less interested, but these values will be reinforced if you are also able to establish a little competition for it. If your friend wants you out of the "friend zone" and in the romantic zone, the competition will not please her. When you stay busy with other people, your friend will crave more of your time and attention. You can start testing this concept using the concept of "social proof." Start posting photos of you with your other friends on your Facebook, to see if that "friend," with whom you are trying to light the flame, tells you something about it.

5. Ask your friend for a favor; Let him invest time in you. An excellent way to measure if your friend wants you to leave the "Friends Zone" and enter the romantic zone is to test her willingness to invest in you. This is a scientific principle that was called the "Ben Franklin" effect by researchers in a 1969 edition of the Human Relations Magazine. The Ben Franklin effect revolves around making people spend more time and attention on you, and in doing so, you become more meaningful to them.

Women are more frequently attracted to men who mean something to them.

Test your willingness to leave the "Friends Zone" by asking her a favor or finding a way for her to invest in you and your life.

She may not jump into romance immediately, but now she will be spending time and attention on you and will be more willing in the future.

The researchers suggest that even asking for something so simple, but intimate, like something from the fridge, will work.

Be it, your friend, or a stranger, appealing to her emotional side will probably work in your favor when you are trying to get out of the "Friend Zone."

Nevertheless, it is also important not to make your friends very easy and attainable. This makes things too comfortable, and she does not have a real motivation to leave the "Friends Zone."

How to fall in love with your best friend - make her fall in love with you!

Falling in love with your best friend is a common thing. Surely, you are already walking there.

Now you want to know how making her fall in love with you. The good news is that you have already accomplished the most difficult.

1-Hard work is made

When it comes to getting a girl, in this case, that your best friend falls in love with you, creating an emotional connection, a sense of trust and security are the hardest things to do.

You have already done this - that is why they are best friends. What needs to be done now is to change the dynamics of your relationship, going from being a trusted friend to the type of man with whom you can see yourself having passion, sex!

2-Set limits

To take her to reciprocate your love, you're going to have to start setting limits.

What this means is that you have to stop being there for all your emotional needs.

For example, if she always goes to you to complain about her love life, it is necessary to set a limit that prevents that.

There does not have to be a big statement; It can be straightforward actions, for example, not responding to your texts or checking your voicemails until you know why you want to talk.

3-Get to flirt

The most significant way you're going to start changing the dynamics of your relationship is flirting. But how to flirt? Here are a couple of tips on how to make it happen the right way:

- **Stay light:** When it comes to flirting, you want to be playful. Think of yourself as a fun little car child. Make her laugh, get her smile, and make her have fun. Do not take it too seriously and do not enter seeking approval or acceptance. Remember that it is a game and the games are supposed to be fun.

- **Dealing with the blows:** When you start joking and flirting, she will make jokes to test you and see how well you react. The good news is that if she is doing this, it means she is interested. You have to roll with her. For example, if she says something like, "What a shame you are so small or else we could go out," you say, "Pity, you are so tall!" You can also say things that deflate the joke like "You are like my sister small - cute, but annoying."

4-Leave her wanting more

Whether you're trying to get your best friend to fall in love with you or a girl you just met, leaving her wanting more is one of the best tools you can have. How do you do that?

- **Appointments:** Encounters for short things that allow the two to have fun together for a specified period. Good examples of this type of dating include going to comedy shows, a round of mini-golf or going to a carnival together.
- **Discussion:** At a high point during the interaction, tell him how well you are having, but no more than twice in a single day. Be sure to tell her that you are attracted to her for reasons other than her appearance.
- **Touch:** Touch dramatically increases intimacy. Its forearms, shoulders, and upper back are very "safe" places where you can touch it. In addition, touching it permits you to start playing.

Combine these three and she will start to miss you a lot when you are not around.

5-Build your trust

It's true: The sexiest thing for a woman is trust.

How to Fall in Love with Your Best Friend - For your best friend to fall in love with you, you will need to build trust.

I know what you're thinking: It's easier said than done.

How to Love Your Best Friend - How you can build your trust. Here's how:

- **Better body language:** Adopting the body language of a safe man will eventually make you feel more confident. Smile a lot and do "body checks" throughout the day: Are you standing with your back straight, for example? You will be surprised at the difference this does and how quickly it does it.
- **Get used to talking to women:** Whenever you have the time, go out and talk to women. It doesn't matter if it's your favorite bar or a strip club: The point is to feel comfortable talking to beautiful women without being shaken. Talk to women without trying to tie them up. Instead, get used to being with them and chat.
- **Act as if:** "Act as if." It is also known as "pretend it until you do it." It is scientifically proven to work. If you want to be a confident man, look around, and see how safe men act. Realize that you have already reached your goal. It will bring you much closer to achieving it.

- **Get physical:** many kids lack confidence because they are not in contact with their bodies. If you are not exercising regularly, do it. Not only is it right for you, but it will make you feel better about yourself. If you have trouble feeling motivated, start going with a friend.
- **Date one quirk:** One way to begin to feel instantly safer is to get some new threads. Dig through men's magazines and then go to the mall or a fashion store. If you are not much about walking well dressed, ask the sales girl for help. Even a new pair of jeans and a shirt can make you feel like a million dollars. Not to mention in a haircut (if you have!).

Only a couple of simple things can begin to unlock the trust you already have inside - and make your best friend fall in love with you.

CHAPTER 7: WHAT FEMALE BODY LANGUAGE MEANS

You know a girl you like. How do you understand if she likes you back?

The old question to determine whether a girl likes a boy is one that has been asked since the beginning of time.

Despite all that time, men have not yet determined what the right time to make a move is and when they need to go back.

A majority of the male population makes a movement too early or too late.

Sure, some Alpha pros are stars in the game, but generally speaking, most men do it wrong.

I know it would be much simpler if the world worked based on a direct standard. Well, it's unfortunate, but it doesn't work that way.

Today, it's all about persecution and the challenge of trying to determine what women want.

Fifteen clues of women's body language that you need to be vigilant.

Unless women are desperate or more than hot or desire for sex, or bored, THEY will not make it easier for you to catch them.

The vast majority of men think that it is not necessary to captivate a woman, yes, the vast majority believe that it is entirely useless, so when they are in a cafeteria, in the library, a football game or a bar, they Like to know that you are paying attention and making an effort to take notes of your signals and clues.

And as ALL women thoroughly enjoy the game of seduction, here are 15 clues of the body language of the women she sends if she likes you.

1 Makes eye contact.

If she makes eye contact with you, especially if it is repeated, she is interested.

Another way to know if she likes you is to take note if she hides, or let's know the fact that she is looking at you.

If she lets you know she's only looking at you, you've already hit a home run.

Two are coming.

Women do not try to approach and get personal with the people they dislike, so if you feel that she is approaching your own space that is a definite clue that she likes.

She will play with you and get close enough, that you are almost touching, then walk away, highlighting the apparent void between you.

She will also make an effort to sit or stand next to you and find small excuses to interact with you in conversation so she can get closer.

3 Makes physical contact.

Similar to the previous point, women-only touches the people they like. If you think about it, this is the case for all people on planet earth.

If she starts to make physical contact with you, you can be sure that she is showing interest.

Take note of the small signs, such as briefly placing your hand on your knee, touching your arm, touching you lightly when she laughs, and others.

Any form of contact is right, even an accidental touch, because you can't prevent her from accidentally touching you so you can touch your abs.

4 She smiles more.

Smiling is one of the most significant indicators when you're trying to determine if a girl likes you. This means that she enjoys your company and does not bother you that you are close.

Take note of how she reacts with others. If she smiles the same and so often, then you may have to look for other clues of interest.

But if you're sure that she treats you with millions of smiles, you already earned it.

5 It focuses on you.

It is basic courtesy to focus on the other person when they have a conversation, and although this is an unmentioned rule, not many people pay attention to it.

I'm sure you've had to deal with rude conversationalists who look all over the place, check their phones and watches, and seem bored in the middle of the conversation.

Well, if the girl you like does that, it is evident that she is not interested.

However, if she is fixed on you, no matter what you say, you can be sure that she is interested.

I have seen MANY women pretend interest in many subjects, to be able to continue talking with a man.

6 Looks at your lips.

If she looks at your lips more than once, she is interested. I can guarantee that she is imagining those lips on theirs and assessing her thicknesses and the ability to please her mouth.

If her eyes focus on your lips with a frequency so that you notice it, trust me when I say she is very interested.

7 Call attention to your lips.

Once she looks on your lips, there is a high possibility that she will imagine them on her own, which will inadvertently lead her to draw attention to her lips.

Take note of seemingly involuntary movements such as applying the lipstick again, biting your lower lip, or running your fingers across your lips.

By the time she begins to call attention to that area, you will know that she is interested.

8 Raise your eyebrows.

This is a relatively gray area, but it is worth checking out. I call it a gray area because a girl who raises her eyebrows does not necessarily mean that it is an indication that she likes you.

This action has to be paired with something else. For example, a raised eyebrow and a smile is a good thing, but a raised eyebrow with pressed lips should be a sign that you should get out of there.

9 Arms at your sides.

As long as she has her arms at her sides, you will have a driveway. This indicates openness and willingness to participate now.

If she crosses her arms, you can be sure that she is involuntarily protecting herself from your seductive moves, so stop trying.

10 He leans toward you.

If she leans toward you, especially when there is no need to do so, she likes you. An example is when she leans toward you with the intention of not being able to hear what you were saying.

11 She releases her hair.

When a woman plays with her hair, she is flirting without realizing it. Look for signs that include running your fingers through your hair, rolling a strand on your finger, pulling your hair back, and much more.

She is trying to show her neck, and before you ignore it, remember that the neck is a beautiful and sensitive part of the woman's body.

In Japanese culture, a woman's neck is very erotic, and glimpses of it should be considered a gift.

12 Push your chest out.

Do you know the saying, "if you have it, show it"? Well, women know that men can't resist when they show their breasts, so if you find her pushing her chest out and drawing attention to her assets, you should take it as a sign that she is interested.

13 Dilated pupils.

In the same way that when children's eyes widen when they get a massive vase of candy, a woman's eyes will do the same when they arrive with a monumental man.

Dilated pupils are something she can't control, so if you notice, take it as a sign that she is unconsciously showing interest and emotion.

14 Flap your eyes.

Yes, a woman who flaps her eyelashes at a man can be a stereotypical sign of flirting, but she is not classified as a stereotype for anything. Make sure you know the difference between a fluttering flutter and a flutter of eyelashes for having something in your eye.

15 Palms flipped.

Another sign that she is interested in you is when you see her palms turned and open. This shows openness and willingness to interact with you while clenched fists are negative.

Keep in mind that you are going to have to evaluate several of the signs mentioned above before being sure that a woman likes you.

How Women Like It - Use Your Male Body Language
I will reveal the secrets of how to like women using your male body language

If you want to know exactly how women like you, you are going to have to become the kind of man they look at in amazement.

I do not know if you know, but your body language speaks more than your voice, yes, and it is much more than your voice; in reality, your male body language speaks 92% and your voice, your words 8%. This is why you have to learn how women like to talk very little, just using your body.

How to Like Women - How can you become with little effort the focus of women's attention?

Have you noticed how the great gallants both in the movies and on TV know perfectly well how women like it?

Well, you also have the potential to create all that aura of male attraction, only with your male body language.

But I get your attention ... You have to be natural, because if you make any movement in which you reflect doubt or nervousness, how it would be to look towards the ground or be with your arms crossed, restlessness, friend.... Women are not going to want to be near you.

Now, think about how these successful kids do it. They do know how to attract girls. In addition, what is their secret? Nothing you can't do... be relaxed and always have the situation under control.

How to Like Women - I know that you know because there are many cases of men who are not handsome nor rich, but they know how to attract women as if they were magnets. I will reveal your Great Secrets:

Secret # 1 For How Women Like It: A Strong, Clean And Good Health State

Instinctively for women, if you have good health, at an unconscious level, they interpret that you are going to give them healthy and strong babies and that by your strength, you will be there for them protecting them.

This is very deep, and above it seems that it has nothing to do ... BUT the health of a man is something so powerful that without them knowing it you can attract many women with this quality, and I repeat, this is on an unconscious level, they do it by natural selection.

And how do they perceive it? Well, they use their eyes and nose; this is how they evaluate your health and what possibilities you have to procreate babies and that these are healthy.

So my recommendation for you is to take care of yourself doing functional exercises, get enough sleep and drink enough natural water, consume healthy foods, and follow a hygiene habit.

Secret 2- For How Women Like To Use Your Male Body Language: Walk, Stop, And Smile Like An All-Star

When you are standing or if you are sitting, but erect with your chest, straight out, with your head straight, and your intestine aspirated, your body is relaxed, not rigid.

These are the positions that suggest that you dominate the situation and that you are a man who has self-confidence; you have great control over yourself, a lot of pride and determination.

Do not do things so fast, because you have to make your movements PAUSE, yes, do it a little more at the pace than usual. You must stay cold all the time, always with your mind in the "SERENA" mode. You know, stroll, and never stop smiling.

Secret 3 For How Women Like It: Become A Leader

Look, when you already know how women like me, I see it as a synonym for natural leadership. One thing that I tell you is that you learn not to ask anyone's approval be yourself.

If you go to a bar or any other place where there are people, walk swaying, with your head always high and never stop smiling.

You have not seen that this is how celebrities act when they are in social. Take a walk as if you were at home, reflect that security.

Another thing is that when you talk to a woman, you won't smile much. What you will do is look into her eyes, and listen to her, understand what she has to say.

But don't forget that it is you who is in charge of that situation. It is You who must have full control of that conversation. Dare to touch him on her arm, in her hand, so she will see that it is you who dominates everything and even her personal space.

Apply it !!!

You have to go out and start right now; you have to be very active in the social scene of your locality!

Keep in mind that you should always be calm and sure of yourself. Do not be afraid of the mistakes you can make because, to be successful, you have to be willing to make mistakes.

Do not apologize to anyone and much less if it is for any nonsense, even if you have made a mistake.

CHAPTER 8: HOW TO CONQUER A WOMAN WITH A BOYFRIEND

Steps to link a girl with a boyfriend. I am not responsible for the consequences that may occur if you achieve the goal.

1- Meet the boyfriend: If you know the people you are competing with, you will have the chance to defeat him.

In the meantime, stay in the shadows, and the grill does not know who you are.

2- Mine the ground: Get in the head of the woman in a subtle but imposing way and mainly in the points that you know weak of the grill of the moment. (Which you already know from the previous point).

Let's go with an example: If the lady complains that her boyfriend does not pay enough attention, do not go out of your way to attend to her ... remember some unexpected detail from a previous conversation with her, and ask her how to follow such a topic. (If it lacks memory, try recording a conversation, with an mp3 it reaches, no need to adhere microphones with tape under the shirt).

Example 2: If she complains that her boyfriend is very jealous, do not tell her, "I would let you do what you want because I like the free thing." In this case, you should not replace that, but feed the ego, semi giving the grill the reason.

Say ... "I understand because you're beautiful... but I should trust you, isn't it the most important thing?". Then change the subject immediately. Follow with: "with ice for you, right?" and move away to look for the drink, leaving her alone meditating.

3- Do not be your confidant: For this advice, there are two main reasons.

a) The boyfriend will automatically believe that it is you who wants to face the girl (and he will be right) because he will no longer be in the shadows and may be subject to the attacks of the youth in question.

b) If you are the confidant, what you will achieve is to prepare the ground for a third jackal or vulture to appear on the scene and reap the sowing that you made.

4 - Do not attack the boyfriend: A beginner's mistake is to attack the current grill since one believes that this will be able to show itself as a better option. It is not the way.

If she says, for example: "Yes, but Joaquin tires me with his persecutions," do not say: "And yes, it is a dummy (no matter how it is)," since it will awaken rebellion and Want to defend it.

5 - Make her angry: Not with something negative, but it is mini anger, generate a situation in which she challenges him, or even hit him softly for something you said. If it is for something disrespectful much better if it is something rude, rogue, and about his figure, more than better. If it is something naughty, mischievous, about his character and that he gets her to blush and hit him much better.

For disrespectful, we speak of a phrase closer to James Bond than to a neo-Cordoba mason, and for rogue, we talk about a smile from a single corner and not humorous to Sofovich's magazine.

6- Have fun and seduce it: Base yourself on those two condiments to devote yourself to a vulture. Something is missing in your relationship and is probably one of those two. Remember the "Too much" rule, why fun is not being your clown, and seducing her is not becoming George Clooney.

7- Challenge her: This means that the situation is that you are the prize, and she alone decides to conquer it.

- **Clarification:** For this, she needs a lot of ingenuity, but in the end, to make her think that everything was her idea.

8- With Security, go!: Finally, when you think you are well advanced and that your chances are sufficient, do not hesitate, attack with all the energy, it may be the only opportunity you have left, and it is time to throw yourself with all the momentum.

CHAPTER 9: WHAT IS THE BEST PERFUME TO ATTRACT WOMEN YOU CAN USE?

In this chapter, I want to talk not only about the type of perfume you should use but about the importance of using perfume in the first place.

Now, it is difficult to recommend something as subjective as a perfume, since everyone has different tastes.

However, when it comes to perfume to attract women, I recommend the following:

- Gucci Nobile
- Armani Code (For me the best fragrance for men and my personal favorite)
- Black Jeans by Versace
- Aqua, by Christian Dior
- Fahrenheit, by Christian Dior

As you can see, these perfumes are some of the leading brands in the market. This is important.

I consider them the best perfumes for men when it comes to attracting women; women are "crazy" with them!

Cheap perfumes are not only going to evaporate faster, but they can be ruined ... that is, the perfume you put on to increase your chances with women can, in fact, potentially ruin your chances.

So do not be tempted to save some money on cheaper options when choosing a perfume.

But top-notch perfumes are costly!

It is true. However, you will realize that they also have a much more reasonable price if you buy them on the Internet than in stores.

Although you have to make sure you're buying from a reputable source and not from someone who traffics goods.

One of the advantages of buying online that also sell samples from different colonies for a minimum fraction of the price of the bottles.

In this way, you can try the different colonies and realize things like:

- How long the essence lasts before it fades away.
- If the essence interacts with your body odor in a way you did not expect.

Yes, you can try the perfumes in the store, but it is better to try them while using them for a couple of hours to try the two aspects mentioned. In this way you can choose a good brand and pay for insurance, knowing that it is the one for you.

How powerful is wearing perfume?

Psychologically speaking - smells have a powerful effect on humans.

Just think about the effect that women's perfume has on you when you approach it - wouldn't you like to produce a similar effect on it?

In addition, considering that it is scientifically proven that women have a more developed sense of smell than men - using a good perfume becomes vital to introduce positive emotions into the woman you have selected.

There is one last advantage of wearing perfume, and most men do not use it! (I mean quality ones)

Therefore, your decision to wear perfume gives you leaps and bounds ahead of other men.

While flirting, it is the little things that make the difference ... and a good perfume is one of those tricks that you will want to take advantage of.

As you learned, using any perfume to try to attract women, is not something you should take lightly, always use a good perfume, even if it costs twice as much as your budget!

EYE, perfume is just one more point when it comes to attracting women, as you present yourself is even more critical, that is, your confidence, security, this makes a BIG difference ...

What are the best pheromones to attract women? It is not what you are thinking!

You can't imagine which are the best pheromones to attract women. Have you ever wondered how that girl fell in love with an egocentric and abusive idiot?

You treated her much better, but of course ... She completely ignores you. Why?

Is it because that guy is using pheromones to attract women while you aren't?

Before continuing my game, I want to tell you that pheromones to attract women DO NOT WORK, they are a scam business... POINT!

This mystery bothers most men. Most of them do not understand why women fall in love with the wrong men ... The bad guys!

So the question is: Why do so many beautiful girls fall in love with arrogant, abusive, and selfish idiots?

It took me many years to find out, but I will share this secret with you. And EYE, it has nothing to do with pheromones to attract women!

If you want to know how and why bad guys attract so many beautiful women, you should put yourself in their shoes and ask yourself...

Why don't those girls go out with good men who treat them like princesses?

They go out with arrogant idiots and bad guys ... and NOT those who are good with them, make them compliments, carry flowers, and want to invite them to dinner.

The first thing you notice now is that being "BAD" gets you ten times more girls than being "GOOD."

Look around and see the couples where the girl is really beautiful and attractive.

Your partner is not exactly the typical "good man."

So how do bad guys do it? What makes them so sexy and attractive to women?

It is because women want to be with a man who represents a challenge, and it is not easy to be with them. Rough guys and idiots don't care if the girl likes them or not, while the good guy is needy, sticky, and desperately wants to date her.

Rough guys are wild; they break the rules and do what they want. Women are automatically attracted to that behavior because it is exciting and unpredictable.

Good guys ALWAYS do predictable things, therefore they are boring to female eyes.

Bad guys are always superior when it comes to conquering and seducing the most beautiful women. Watch celebrities. They can choose any man ... and who do they end up with?

They end up with an alcoholic rocker, a "bad guy" actor, or an abusive idiot with his whole body tattooed.

But what attracts women towards these types is not abusive behavior, arrogance, or tendencies of family violence ... Of course not.

You see, if you were a woman and you had to choose between a good man who has nothing else to offer but the perfect date like going to a restaurant where he pays for everything or a movie where he buys you chocolate and flowers ... then here the woman prefers the OTHER guy.

And that, sadly, is the bad guy on the block.

You hear many people comment that this type of man is "the wrong man," but what else is there?

Let's keep thinking as a woman friend....

As a woman, you always choose the wild man, rebellious, and in love with himself over the kind and stupid guy who would do anything for you.

Think about it.

I think you realized ... stop thinking about pheromones to attract women and start being more rebellious, wild, and have priorities over women.

The best pheromones to attract women is that you be a man who is hard, rebellious, wild!

CHAPTER 10: WHY DO WOMEN LIKE BAD MEN?

Some time ago, I saw a study that demonstrated - once again - one thing that we seduction experts have known for a long time: the attraction that women feel for bad boys.

I summarize this, what he wants to tell us is that first of all this is a reasonably logical statement: for a man who loves himself, has many more options than those who have little or no confidence in himself, and this "bad" boy "He will never let any woman dominate his life, and this is the type that in our society is considered to be the masculine type - and VERY attractive - and the other the" good one "is nothing more than the one that the typical great payer The one that will always be controlled. The latter does not know how to conquer a woman.

Because of Women Like Bad Men - An Uncomfortable Truth.

The point is that the good boy does not have that something that the bad boy does have: these "bad" boys bring emotions to the lives of women; believe me, these guys are very scarce.

These guys will always be a challenge for women, they are not submissive, do not confuse me with evil to that man who aggravates them physically or insults him, if he is not the type that always makes women bend, break, cry and suffer them missing them because they can't have them the way they want.

There is an actual little accepted by women, and this truth which is said in some surveys is, that they (women) said when asked what kind of men they prefer, they expressed that "I like them to be understanding, gentlemanly and sensitive and always be there for me".

Friend, I will tell you that this is FALSE, and it is not that they are lying, not at all, it is merely that they are confusing how they would like men to be, with how they are the men who attract them.

You copy me, well many knows, but they love this kind of "good boy" to take advantage of it.

"According to these studies, it is also shown that women find it very difficult to resist these types of bad men. And the secret of his success is based on three dominant personality traits, which can incredibly have our friend James Bond as an example.

Because of Women Like Bad Men - Traits

These three powerful personality traits of a bad guy are: an obsession with themselves... they are narcissistic, have psychopathy of being insensitive, impulsive and always looking for risk, and the disappointing exploitative nature of a Machiavellian.

This may not sound pretty, but this is very rare and incredibly sound or may seem, these traits for women equate a lot with masculinity and the ability to raise healthy babies.

That is to say, because of Because Women Like Bad Men, it goes beyond the pure desire to the difficult, from what cannot be as they want, this is internally genetic. Surprise!

I wait for hurdles understanding what I just told you, this bad guy goes after the girl who knows he has chemistry towards him, when he talks to the girls he takes care that the girl shoots the level of attraction to him, the bad boy makes her feel sexually attracted to him.

This guy is one of the men who catch his eye with something creative, unique, this kind of bad boy keeps the woman from the fire, his burning flame, since he knows how to do it, and this is achieved by telling her what She wants to listen.

Why Women Like Bad Men - Chemistry

You may think what you want, but the "bad guys" are never wasting their time with women who are not interested in them.

They know how to accept rejection, they look for another, another one in which if a point of interest is found between them, then from that point, he moves to achieve the goal.

Do not misunderstand me, if you do not want to go so fast you have the freedom to concentrate and strive in only one woman, but friend, if this girl is not in you, if she is not at all interested in you, then you have to wake up and pass tab... Say this, the following.

If you know why women like bad men, you will understand me.

You have to be tough if you want to know how to dominate a woman!

Well, friend, I know you know this, but I will repeat it, one thing is that you are a boy dedicated to a woman and another is that you are a stupid total that all he does is waste his time and money with a woman who does not love you.

The "bad boys" will always go full load in these cases, and they will only devote more time to those battles they know they can win and if they are worth it if they don't say, THE OTHER!

Is this about him Because Women Like Bad Men, is it awful?

Because Women Like Bad Men is not a bad thing in itself.

As I told you, this is a sign of masculinity, and that they can give their offspring a better quality of life than a submissive guy.

This type of man also knows how to arouse lust in a woman, he creates confidence, and they disinhibit them in sex, he knows how to get that female fierce locked up by the bars of society. This guy knows what they want in a man.

6 Reasons Why Eye Contact Is Great When Seducing Women

Some of us make a lot of eye contact, but most of us don't do enough.

Whether you're a single or married man, eye contact can be a powerful social tool from the office to the bar.

Here, in this section, we teach that eye contact is one of the fundamental keys to the creation, maintenance, and deepening of attraction and sympathy. Here is why.

You can study about eye contact (or lack thereof), to see what is essential for the person you are talking to. To put it bluntly, if a woman is interested, you will get a lot of eye contact from her.

Eye contact builds trust
A Northwestern University study, published in the Journal of Participatory Medicine, observed 110 interactions for the first time between doctors and patients. They discovered that patients whose doctors had more significant eye contact with them had more confidence with their doctors than those who did not have as much eye contact with their doctors.

So, while the popular idea that lack of eye contact means that a person is lying is just a myth, it doesn't matter. The fact that people perceive those who do not make much eye contact as unreliable people is essential. And it is not a good omen for those who avoid looking into each other's eyes.

The eyes are the windows of the soul

I encourage men to smile and not only with their mouths, but with their whole faces, especially their eyes. There is a bit of science behind that; an MIT study found that babies follow the eyes and not the movements of the adults' heads to know what is essential.

Similarly, you can study eye contact (or lack thereof) to understand what is essential to the person who is speaking. To put it bluntly, if a woman is interested in you, she will have a lot of eye contact with you.

Eye contact communicates Intelligence

It is a fact that you are more likely to get a job if you make eye contact during the job interview. We believe that the reason is that you communicate intelligence and competence through the eyes. The study linked above found another interesting fact: the more intelligent and competent you are, the less you have to make eye contact. So you can stop reading this, Mr. Clooney.

Eye contact is sexy

A team of psychologists from the University of Aberdeen discovered that a happy face making direct eye contact is perceived as much more attractive than a pleasant-looking face avoiding eye contact.

This is how the study was conducted: Participants were shown images of members of the opposite sex smiling, frowning, looking straight ahead, and looking away. As it turned out, they prefer less attractive people who looked directly at them than more beautiful people who did not look at them.

This highlights the fact that attractiveness is much more than physical appearance. Confidence, charisma, and warmth can take you far.

Eye contact decreases hostility

Here is a rare study with some real-life applications: people are hateful on the Internet because they are not making eye contact with the people they are talking to. The study was conducted at the University of Haifa and was published in the journal Human Behavior.

The participants were seated in a room to hold a debate. One group shared personal information about themselves, while others had to maintain direct eye contact with the people they were listening to. When eye contact was not being made, participants were twice as hostile as when it was being made.

The personal information did not have the same weight either. So when you encounter some resistance or even hostility, making eye contact can make all the difference in the world. Eye contact fosters empathy and a greater sense of emotional understanding, which is quite challenging to ignore.

Eye contact confers character

Here is one last study that is a bit strange and contradictory. Eye contact shows that you trust the abilities of others. In a study published in the Journal of Non-Verbal Behavior, researchers reported that if your boss has a lot of eye contact with you, it means he thinks a lot about you. This can be applied in other places: When you are in a bar, talking to a woman, making eye contact gives you status, assuming that is something you want to happen, of course.

CHAPTER 11: POSTURES TO ATTRACT A WOMAN

These are some positions to attract a woman, and you will learn about your body language

As you may know or perhaps learn, it is estimated that 67% to 93% of our human communication is nonverbal (according to university researchers) and that with your body language, you can reveal your internal emotional state. Whether you have had a terrible day or you have won the lottery. This means that you can know what emotions someone is feeling by observing his or her body language, without that person even having to say a word.

Therefore, you, as a man who is trying to lift and seduce women, have necessarily pay close attention to what you are communicating nonverbally.

Learning body language consists of the following, pay attention to the postures to attend a woman:

- Your Way of Moving. Move as if nothing, your movements must be carefree; you must act as if you were so but so successful that you rarely have a reason to hurry or impress someone (you are a person who has nothing to prove because you already have it everything... think so at least!). Move around the world doing what you want, and assuming that others will follow; this is pure law of attraction.

- Body displacement. Spread your arms and legs. Do not be intimidated; you can take up all the space around you, sit in your house wherever you are.

- **Your voice.** It should have a calm, softening, and dominant effect. Try not to speak too loudly and much less quickly.

- **Your face.** The facial muscles always keep them relaxed. Never tense your jaw, and only rarely, should you frown or wrinkle your eyebrows.

- **Your shoulders.** Position your shoulders as if you had just received a good massage. Do not lift them, as you will notice yourself as a nervous person.

I will be something extreme with you now, but I want you to understand the Importance of Body Language that I would dare to say that your body language is more important than anything you usually say to women, and this is because every word that comes out of Your mouth will necessarily have to match your body language, if this is not the case then you will not succeed with women.

I explain myself if you tell stories to a woman who transmits your confidence, but at the same time you sink and cross your arms, then you will notice that you are false.

You know that with my body language, I have managed to get up women in the past, YES, only with writing. A couple of months ago, I was in a cafeteria where I usually go, lounging on the couch, arms open, feet on the table.

The mental attitude I had was that I felt so comfortable that it was as if I was at home resting on my sofa. It was as if he owned the cafeteria.

The net result was that a girl sitting near me lowered her book and began a random trivial talk.

IMPORTANT (When an attractive woman you do not know, randomly, seeks conversation with you, you should ALWAYS assume that she feels attracted to you. It will sound somewhat arrogant, but that is what you must be proud to a point, they like to them, but you must always assume that they are for you if this condition happens to you. This is logical to think about, and this is because women do generally not risk all the masculine-feminine dynamics, and even more especially with a stranger, unless they feel attraction)

The main point here is that she was initially attracted to me, and then she approached me because of my body language.

Now, of course, body language is not enough. You should also have an internal mental attitude of an alpha male that is consistent with your body language.

However, do not make mistakes, as if your body language conveys confidence, then your mood will also change to make you safer. In addition, did you ever notice how, when you walk with a jump in your step, do you feel livelier?

On the contrary, when you lower your eyes and drag your feet, you feel depressed. Then your mental attitude also follows the body language you adopt.

So, in conclusion, be an alpha male with your mental attitude and body language. It is in a woman's personal space and be sexual and interested in her, but at the same time, do not show that you need affection or desperate for her attention. Just comfortable and enjoy it.

Moreover, when your body language transmits that, it means that later on you will be comfortable and enjoying... with the woman. Well, I hope you understand that the positions to attract a woman are mandatory when it comes to flirting.

CHAPTER 12: PHRASES TO INVITE A WOMAN OUT

Exchanging text messages with a woman through the numerous messaging applications that currently exist, such as WhatsApp, Facebook Messenger, Line, Telegraph, Skype, or even the less and less used SMS messages, is an art. Of course, it is not space science, but if you want to do it well and that she does not end up not responding to your messages as it happens with 8 out of 10 men who send messages improvised, and then you have to know what you are doing.

Conquering a woman is a three-step process that begins by creating attraction, continues to make her feel comfortable and at ease in your company, to finally move towards romance and seduction.

This three-step process also works in the virtual world, and text messages must conform to this process. This is what Bobby Rio calls *La Sequencia Cerrojo*, which is nothing more than these three steps, but adapted to the art of messages to conquer a woman by cell phone.

In this chapter, I will discuss something more concrete: How to create phrases to invite a woman out and send them through instant messaging. Also, I will share with you some of the best phrases to invite a woman out; these phrases can be sent separately or embedded within a broader message that you can send via WhatsApp, Line, Facebook Messenger, SMS, or any other messaging system.

The phrases to invite a woman out that I am going to share with you throughout this chapter have proven their effectiveness with different people and in different situations, but still; they are not one hundred percent infallible. Your success will depend on you, sending them to the right woman at the right time.

If you send a message containing one of these phrases to invite a woman out before she is ready to accept your invitation, you will get a negative or eternal silence, if you do it later, you will have lost time, and your willingness to accept has probably decreased. That is why you must know how to choose the best moment, and this is something you will be able at once you will finish reading this book. And maybe you will experience a high impulse to take your cell phone and send a message to the girl you like so much and you are experiencing a crazy and robust desire to go out with.

How to invite a woman out using text messages

I still have not mentioned what the right moment is, that is something we are going to discover together in the next lines.

The right time to send a message containing these phrases to invite a woman out is when you have managed to generate enough attraction in her to want to date you, and enough confidence to feel safe dating you. This is truer today than ever, when the stories of counterfeiting and phishing are present everywhere. This makes sense because if he does not like you, he will not want to go out with you, and if he likes you but does not trust you, he won't risk it either.

That is why I mentioned that seduction is a process and that text messages to conquer a woman must conform to that process.

If you are trying to ask a woman out using messages, that means you have her phone number, which may fit into one of the following two scenarios:

The first scenario is the one where you met a girl, approached her, talked, and she gave you her phone number because of the intervention. The second is the one in which you know the girl because she is your friend, or a work or school partner.

The two scenarios I have just mentioned are those that occur most frequently when you try to invite a woman out using messages, and what they have in common is that both lack one of the two elements I mentioned earlier. In the first scenario, she gave you her phone number because she wants to keep in touch with you, which means that there is some attraction. However, you have only been with her once, and she still does not know you enough, so she does not have yet enough trust. In the second scenario, the girl lives with you frequently, which means that there is enough confidence, but little or no attraction.

Therefore, the first thing you should do if you want to invite a girl out by message is to determine in which case you are, determine what exists and what is missing. Not all cases are the same if there is enough attraction, but trust is limited, focus on building trust; If, on the contrary, there is trust but no attraction, your goal should be to create appeal.

How to use messages to attract a woman

Let's start with the second scenario, the one where you have a girl's phone number because it's a friend, a neighbor, a school or work colleague, or you know her from somewhere; You have frequent contact with her, and there is trust, but no attraction. Your goal, in this case, should be to create attraction, and text messages work very well in this case.

First, think about those things that make men attractive, and if you think it all comes down to being so handsome that you look like Brad Pitt's clone, think twice. What women find attractive in a man is sexual value, which is a combination of elements, and personality traits, in which physical appearance counts, but only 10 or 15 percent at most. This is very good news, because you do not need to be very handsome to be attractive, but you do need to have confidence in yourself, fun character, intelligence, social proof (having many people seeking your attention, if they are much better women), mystery, leadership, ambition, and something that makes you different from others (attractive differentiation).

Your messages and phrases to invite a woman out should reflect these traits, but without saying openly that you are sure of yourself, or that you are funny, you should only express it subtly in your messages, and if she tells you that you are the, You have won.

For example, imagine that you send a message like the following:

"Hey, you! If you! You know to keep a secret?"

What do you think will happen?

In the first place, as she already knows you, this will seem fun, and you are appealing to the mystery and arousing her curiosity because she senses that you are about to tell her a secret. She is so curious that she will answer YES. Then you continue writing:

"Don't tell anyone, but I met an overwhelmingly cute girl the other day. Her name is (put her name here in uppercase). It's a shame that..."

Now you have let her know that you consider her pretty, but you are not kissing the ground she steps on, on the contrary, you are creating mystery and encouraging her to answer you. I can bet you that she will wait a few minutes, and see that you are not writing anything else; she will write to you to ask, "Pity what?"

Which means you are making her feel interested. Now she knows you like her, and she is showing interest in knowing more. You are growing in it, you are making it think of you, and that stimulates the attraction.

How To Use Messages To Build Trust In A Woman

Now let us go to the first case, the one in which a woman finds you attractive but still doesn't trust you enough to go out alone. This may happen because he has just met you or because he doesn't know enough about you yet.

It is easier to build trust than to create attraction; this is because the attraction starts from zero, while trust is built based on the attraction. Nevertheless, let us go in parts:

We said that self-confidence is one of the qualities that women find most attractive in a man, confidence is synonymous with security, and if you are sure the woman senses that you are trustworthy, which makes things easier for you.

But if you doubt, if you go around, if you ask too many questions, if your messages by message seem more like an interrogation than a fun interaction between two people who like each other, she can conclude that there is something strange about you, making her feel insecure and leading her to lift the guard. Avoid this, and you will create trust very quickly.

When you are with her face to face, trust is built by climbing levels of intimacy through physical contact. In-text messages, however, you cannot touch it. The only thing you can do in this case is, to be honest, and go straight to the point, even better if in your messages you use words that evoke trusts, such as sincerity, honesty, no doubt, or loyalty; since those words generate emotions of confidence and security at the unconscious level.

Let's put the following message as an example:

"Let's be honest. I know that you like me and you know that I like you. What we do about it?"

or

"Honestly? I like you. You are too funny and too cute too. So let's go somewhere together now! "

Most of the so-called seduction gurus claim that you should not be so direct, but we are in the fields of virtual seduction, and the rules change a bit. You need to be straightforward to show that you are being honest and are not hiding anything, that she can trust you.

Believe me when I tell you that women love this kind of honesty because it is.

Phrases to invite a woman out

Now that you have created enough attraction and confidence, it is time to achieve your purpose of dating her, for which you can use the following phrases to invite a woman out, which you can send directly in your messages, or include them in of words that are more significant:

We have been sending messages for a few days, and it has been very nice. Now let's do what ordinary people do and have a drink somewhere where we can talk a little more.

Hey, I know these great places where they have (something you know she likes) Let's go tomorrow!

You seem to be the type of person who has firm ideas and likes to have fun, just like me. So let's have some fun going out to (some fun place) tomorrow!

You know what? If you promise to be my tour guide tomorrow when I am in (a place she knows). I will give you some lessons (something you know how to do) as a reward.

Are you bored? Well, if you play your cards correctly, I could take you to a great place where they will have (something she likes) today in the afternoon.

Aren't you doing anything right now? Then let me take you to (a fun place) where they will have the best (something she likes) that you've never tried!

Hey, my friends and I will spend the afternoon in a friendly place, if you want to come you are invited.

Party to my house at 5 PM! Be sure to bring my favorite wine, or I will send you back.

CHAPTER 13: HOW TO CHAT WITH A GIRL TO CONQUER HER

Something our readers have been asking us very often lately is how to chat with a girl to conquer her.

In addition, it is that chat sites abound, enter Google and place the word chat as search criteria. I did it, and the system threw me a total of ... 12,840,000,000 pages!

Can you believe it? Twelve thousand eight hundred and forty million chat pages!

Add to this the other chat options, such as social networks or cell phone messaging systems and it turns out that there should be no person, man or woman, with no plans to go out for a weekend.

However, the reality is very different. It turns out that 99 out of 100 times that a man contacts a woman by chat comes to nothing. It usually happens that they chat for a while, but then she stops responding to his messages. It also happens that they chat in that session, but there are no more chat sessions between them. Chatting during several sessions is less frequent, but it also happens; In that case, everything ends in pure virtual friendship, and they never get to know each other personally.

In this chapter, I will show how to achieve this: Contact a girl by chat, meet her, maintain permanent contact with her, meet her personally, and conquer her. If you cannot meet personally with the girl you have met by chat, you will only have wasted your time; it is that easy.

It is time to get into the subject, so let's start!

How To Chat With A Girl To Conquer Her

When it comes to conquering a girl by chat, the first step is obviously to enter a chat site and choose the room where you can find the type of woman you are interested in meeting. Most chat sites classify their rooms by age, country, and even personal tastes and interests.

However, in my experience, chat sites are no longer what they were because they have lost ground to chat services placed on social networks such as Facebook since there you can chat with familiar people. In my opinion, if you are looking for new girls you can enter Google and place the word chat as a search criterion, you have more than one thousand two hundred million pages to choose from, so... go ahead!

However, if you are more selective, let's say you want to chat with a woman you like, find a girl with whom you have a mutual friendship, or just see the photo and have more details of the girl you are going to contact; in that case it is more advisable to use Facebook chat.

Nevertheless, before writing even a single word in the Facebook chat, you have to prepare your profile; remember that the profile is your cover letter, and therefore, you must prepare it carefully. Keep in mind that when you send a friend request to the girl you want to contact, she will be curious about who you are, and most likely, she will visit your profile for more information about you. Refine your profile with special care in the following aspects:

Visual elements

Visual elements are the first thing that attracts attention to your Facebook profile, so choose them carefully. There are two visual elements that you should pay much more attention to the profile picture and the header image.

Profile picture:

The image of you will appear not only in your profile but also in each post that you post within the social network. You must put a picture of your face, and pay attention to choosing one where you look perfect; if you are wearing something red (shirt, tie or sweater) much better, because the red color makes you look more attractive. This has a biological basis because it has been proven that in many species of primates the face is reddened as a way of showing willingness to sex and mating. If you are not wearing something red, then place a red frame on your picture.

Cover image:

The photo will appear at the top of your Facebook profile, the ideal size of the cover image is 2120 x 1192 pixels. Here the idea is to place an image of you living with other people at a party, or traveling through a beautiful place, or practicing some extreme sport (football does not count as an extreme sport, eye) or with a lovely friend. This is because this evokes the aspects that are most attractive to women: social friction, leadership, adventure, preselection, etc. There is a lot of time ahead, so soon we will talk about these aspects in this chapter, do not worry.

If you don't have any image like this you can search for a cover for Facebook on the web, there are many websites where you can download Facebook covers ready to upload to your profile, such as Facebook Cover or cover.biz. Although there is a wide variety of cover images, I recommend one of those with positive messages of love or improvement. This type of cover is beautiful to girls because it arouses positive emotions in them and makes them perceive you as a sensitive man with a future. The following images are an excellent example of this type of cover:

Several contacts:

The number of contacts you have has a direct effect on your success when it comes to contacting a person you do not know, especially when trying to chat with a girl you like. Why?

Imagine you create your profile, you have zero friends and contact her. What could she think?

Naturally, she will think about a fake profile created to contact her. Maybe you are a potential stalker, a criminal, or something worse. In this world so full of danger, do you think it will accept your friend request? Of course, the safest thing she can do to avoid any potential issues is to leave your request unaccepted, but she might even block you permanently, and in this case no new requests can be sent.

Now, imagine that you send her a friend request; she visits your profile and finds that you have hundreds of friends of both sexes, of different ages and nationalities. You share things with them, there are many images of you published in your profile, and you also have at least one friend in common with her. This will obviously make her feel more confident and more willing to accept your request.

That is why I highly recommend that before trying to chat with a woman you like on Facebook, you make enough contacts within the network to go through a famous and active person within the site. Of course, you can always buy 500 new friends on Facebook for only 5 dollars, pure boots. It seems tempting, but I do not recommend it; it is still better to have real friendships that interact with you because they will provide you with more opportunities to meet and contact new people, real people.

Network activity:

Quality visual elements and a good number of friends in the network are vital when it comes to chatting with a woman, but the activity in the network is significant as well. Post often, and try to post interesting things like phrases, photos, and videos. Stay active, and you will be more visible.

Now, contact the girl you like...

The next step, after all the previous preparations, is to start contacting beautiful women, if there is a girl in particular that you like this is the time to contact her. Use the Facebook search engine to locate the girl you like by name, or choose the name of your city to find thousands of girls from your locality; Remember that the goal is to know them personally, so there is no point looking in distant towns, much less in countries other than yours. Find women from your city, and it will be easier to have a personal meeting.

Be very careful with the message you send, because by writing that message and sending it you are starting to chat with a woman you like. Two are the goals you absolutely have to reach: catch her interest and curiosity and have your message replied, hopefully as soon as possible.

How to catch woman's interest and chat without boring her

The number one mistake that most men make when chatting with a woman they like is annoying her. Always remember this: if you bore her, she will stop responding to any message you send her, and you will hardly have another chance to contact her virtually as much as in the real world. Under these conditions, you can forget any seduction opportunity

Women respond to emotion, to chat with a woman without boring her you must make her experience intense emotions, you must create what some call "emotional roller coaster," which is nothing more than combining emotions at different degrees of intensity. The number one emotion is laughter, make her have fun while chatting with you, and she won't want to stop chatting. Other emotions are joy, desire, excitement, love, passion, etc.

That's why I recommended you put a profile cover with a phrase of love or overcoming because those phrases arouse emotion. Likewise, every word you write should arouse an emotion. If there is no emotion in your words, they will get bored.

How to make your message replied as soon as possible

A beautiful woman receives a large number of messages through social networks, so if you want her to respond to that first chat, you must place a "hook". This can be achieved in many ways, but in my opinion, the best one is to arouse her curiosity about you by giving some information, but not the whole image. Women are curious by nature, and once they fall into the hook of interest, they are hooked and do anything to know.

Example:

"Hi, how are you?

Remember me? I'm Arthur; we met in Rome, I think... Or was it in Paris?

Well, the fact is that I am sure to meet you, and if you were not there, then you have a double.

I sent you a friend request, I have something to tell you, but first I want to make sure you are the person I'm looking for, and not a double. "

Do you notice how this message plays with the girl's curiosity from the beginning?

If she has been to Rome or Paris, she will wonder who I am and if she met me. If he has never been there, he will be thinking about the double; he will also ask what I have to say. However, she has been hooked through her natural curiosity, and she will have no choice but to accept my request and answer my message if she wants to have all the data and satisfy her curiosity, which will never be completely satisfied. This is personal advice: Never fulfill a woman's curiosity one hundred percent never give her all the pieces of the puzzle and you will keep her following like a nail to a magnet.

How to chat with a woman you like
Chatting with a woman and generating attraction in her is very easy as long as you think outside the box, without asking the same thing that everyone else asks or answering the same thing that everyone else responds. It is painful at first, but it becomes comfortable with practice. Do not hurry too much to ask or answer; this is not a face-to-face conversation, so you can take the time to meditate on your words.

What to ask a girl?

Anything but the classic: "What do you do for a living? How have you been? Do you have a boyfriend?" That kind of thing. You know!

You can ask more original and close to them by just browsing their profile and locating common interests; Facebook provides you with enough information, look at their interests, pages that follow, movies they like, places where they have been. Make a list of all that, and you will find a lot about what to ask.

For example, if you find that she has been in Puerto Rico, you might ask: "Hey, I saw that you have been in Puerto Rico; tell me, what places have you visited?"

This can give a conversation of several minutes on the same subject because as they are passionate topics, she will not stop talking (well, writing) until her fingertips get red.

What to answer to a girl?

Answering is even more fun. When she asks you something, do not hurry to answer, first consider if you can give a funny and emotionally stimulating response. Of course, you will provide her with the answer, but first, you will make her laugh until she loses her breath, which is quite important too. Example:

- She: And what do you do for a living?
- You: I make babies at home.
- She: Hahaha. Seriously!
- You: Seriously, do you want a free sample?
- She: Hahaha. Now, get serious!
- You: Heh, heh. I was kidding. I am a lawyer.

Giving this type of response, you will keep always laughing, stimulating it emotionally and even sexually; and best of all, you'll never get bored.

What follows next?

I recommend you not to chat with her more than three times; the ideal is a couple of times at the maximum. Try to get your phone number as soon as possible and move towards the text message strategy through WhatsApp. In this section, you will find a lot of valuable information about it, to quickly climb to higher levels of intimacy, promptly go out with her and start a relationship.

Isn't it great? Now you know how to chat with a girl you like, without getting bored, awakening beautiful emotions in her from the first moment, awakening a great interest in you, and avoiding becoming a virtual friend. The goal is to chat with the girl you like no more than three times and immediately get her phone number to move the communication to the next level, which is text messages through WhatsApp or another messaging system. Once there, you will begin to send more and more sexy and daring messages to invite her out finally and start the stage of personal encounters, which will lead you to have a relationship with her, whether permanent or temporary.

CHAPTER 14: THE ADVANTAGES OF DATING A SINGLE MOM

Failure seems to be an inherent quality of romance. Just thinking of all the people, we have dated in our lives, how many of them were worth it to get to a second date? The love works under a scheme similar to that of trial and error, which tried any number of options until you find one that more or less satisfies us, and at the same time, we will we fulfill it. It also involves a dose of luck to run into someone attractive, intelligent, interesting, exciting, and, most importantly, compatible.

In that tireless quest to find something similar to love, failures happen at a higher rate than success stories and, many of them can leave sequels that are simply unavoidable. By own decision or by accident, a couple can get pregnant and after the dissolution of the same, regardless of the time that lasted, millions of women remain in the place where they started, only this time with the most significant responsibility to which they will face in their lives: to train a new human being.

According to the National Institute in Mexico, there are about 5.3 millions of moms that raise at least one child alone, either because they are single, divorced, separated, or widowed. The figure is alarming when we look at the rest of our continent, according to a study conducted by the University of Sabana in Colombia: "In South America, more than half of the children born are from single mothers, with the highest rate in Colombia (84 %) " That means that of ten South American children, only five have both parents. For its part, the National

Survey of Occupation and Employment (ENOE) indicates that the highest economic participation rate occurs among single mothers (71.8%), divorced (71.7%) and separated (68.3%), that is, almost seven out of ten works.

In front of us, there is an undeniable reality: in the country, there are 5.3 million women who are perfect candidates to sustain a relationship with them. Although it may soon sound like a monumental and unattractive problem, it is time to remove the stigma that these tireless fighters have had to suffer for decades. Let us then list some of the significant advantages of dating a single mother:

Less drama

Men complain all the time about small fights. Of those minimum incidents that lead to a tidal wave of lawsuits and claims. If a woman has learned something that brings forward one or more children alone, it is to have priorities. They do not want to find a partner to have someone to face because he arrived half an hour late, or because he has not bathed watching a football game. No, they need a person to share fragments of life with, who teaches them a lighter side that makes them laugh, forget about their routine, an adventure companion, and not a boxing bag. They already have enough problems to get one more

An endless source of admiration.

Falling in love arises from the most trivial things like the color and shape of the eyes, the length of the legs, the way someone laughs, their small flaws, or what they like to eat. However, unlike the emotions that will eventually disappear, love is a feeling that is rooted in experiences of higher intensity and scope. The story of a single mother will always be full of fearsome passages that span a range from pain and desolation to violence and survival, but all of them have a common factor: much, much courage. Facts that one cannot believe happened when sitting face to face with its protagonist, but more importantly, seeing it with such courage.

They know what they want.
We have all been with a girl inside a boutique and department store, waiting for her to leave a fitting room while she puts on and removes hundreds of clothes and outfits. Giving our opinion when required, and although not, we are forbidden from going to another establishment to hang out. For some reason, your indecision has to be accompanied. When they finally leave, they receive us with a phrase like: "I didn't like anything, everything looks horrible to me, we go to such a place, and surely there I will find something."

A woman who is a mother has developed a new sense, that of resorting to the practical. He values his time much more, respects that of others, but above all, he has a clear idea of what he needs. In romantic or sexual terms, this makes everything easier: if what you are looking for is a boyfriend, you do not necessarily want a father for your child or, if you are going to have a lover, you will not be involved in the activities in which your child is related.

So the next time you're in front of a girl, and if at any time she shows you the picture of her son (s) on the screen of her mobile phone, instead of getting up and running away from the place, you better stay And know her. Chances are you have the strongest and most interesting woman in your life in front of you.

CHAPTER 15: CHEST HAIR - IS IT ATTRACTIVE TO WOMEN?

In this chapter, I will tell you about the hairs on the chest so that you learn to recognize if they are attractive to women.

Many men have chest hair, and this is very natural in all of us, but that doubt always arises: will this appeal to the women we are with? Well, in this chapter, I will help you clear that mystery to decide on your physical appearance in this regard.

This has long been the subject of debate among women and even among many of us men. Even a few years ago, it was doubtful that a woman would like a man with hair on her chest, but today that phrase "the man is like the bear, the more hairy, the more beautiful" has gained strength. That is where this contradiction is generated that we will deal with today. Are you a man with many hairs on his chest? Alternatively, do you usually shave in that area to appear always very clean? Today you will discover which of the two options suits you best when it comes to appealing to a woman. Let us begin:

It is still a matter of "likes."

You must have this clear before you start with anything, there will be women who find their chest hair attractive and others who will not even want to see it, that is so.

That is why you should get the idea that, although in recent years there has been a tendency of "metrosexual" men who shave all their body, there will also be room for men who have those hairs on their chest, so you should not feel bad about it, or "out of fashion" or anything like that.

Women who prefer chest hair and their reasons

As I mentioned earlier, it should be because there are women with different tastes, and the idea is not to have to change physically to try to please someone. However, you ask yourself, what do women think are attracted to the hair on their chest? What made them have that taste for "hairy men"? Well, let us talk a little about it.

Women are attracted to men with hair on their chest because they find it somehow more manly, mature, and "male," that partner who gives off masculinity and makes them feel protected and cared for.

Although this is beneficial for you, as extra advice I can recommend that you do not accumulate an excessive amount of hair on the chest since many women have stated that it can be uncomfortable for them and look a little unsightly in you when wearing shirts or T-shirts or even in summer you can suffer from excessive sweating. So make sure you have the right amount of chest hair, which is usually about the height of hair that is not uncomfortable for you or your partner, you can take a tight shirt as a measure and see if the hairs are noticeable too much on it , you will know that the hair is already too long. To get that extra game of "masculinity" that conveys so that this type is more attractive to this type of woman.

Those who prefer that hairless area and their reasons

A study at a university in Slovakia set out to compare men with a lot of chest hair with hairless men and no hair on their chest to see which one was more attractive to women. To this end, they brought together two groups of women from Turkey and Slovakia. The result was that only 20% of the women who participated said that a man with hair was attractive and sexual; the rest preferred them without hairs. In addition, there is a large group of women who prefer them that way.

Do you wonder why there are women who prefer hairless men? Well, generally, these are the women who are those fanatics of the "clean," the hair removal, and the care of themselves. They look for men with this type of care and feel attracted to them more easily.

Apart from being more attractive to this group of women, being without hair on the chest also means advantages for you such as, for example, being able to wear any shirt without your hair coming out or getting noticed through it, being able to look better your pecs, always be cold in the heat of summer, etc.

As I mentioned at the beginning of the chapter, all this is a matter of taste. The important thing is that you do not try to change your physique flatly to try to please a woman since there will be one that is very attractive to her chest hair (if you have one) and others that will feel more comfortable if you are somewhat lame (if is that you are)

Feel happy and confident about your appearance, and you will be attractive to women, that is, having hair or not, will not define how attractive you are to a specific group of women. Think about this example: are you one of those who likes women with big tits or big butt? Well, this is precisely what happens with chest hair; it is something that does not matter, something secondary, and that you have to show confidence in yourself and how you are to be attractive to a woman.

CONCLUSION

It is likely men make mistakes on the first date due to lack of experience. Here you will see which are the most significant and most common that can happen to us.

The first date is always a minefield where many things can go wrong if you are not in your five senses.

There is a high probability that you will find your better half, but you are not saved from making any of the most common mistakes on a first date and end up ruining your opportunities.

So that you know them and avoid committing them, I will show you below a small compilation of these.

1. Arrive late

This is one of the most appreciated virtues by any woman and it is unfortunately less and less common nowadays.

Punctuality is something that will help you a lot in every aspect of your life, and dating is no exception.

It does not matter if your girl is late, you have fulfilled your obligation as a man, and you will be there if she is also punctual.

If you have any last-minute inconvenience and you know that you will not be able to arrive on time, you must call or write to your girl to let her know.

2. Do not make decisions

A quality highly valued by women is the security and confidence to make decisions.

Women love men who take the initiative and do not expect them to decide everything.

Asking questions like "Where do you want to go?" "What would you like to do?" "Do you think it's okay if...?", These are things that usually break your nerves if you say it all the time and make you look like A weak and submissive man.

3. Don't take care of your conversation topics

First, you should not make the mistake of staying silent because the last thing you want is to bore your girl. Nevertheless, there are specific conversation topics that you should avoid touching on a first date.

We can find among them: your previous relationships, controversial issues, your shortcomings, work, etc.

You should also avoid getting fed up with questions about her or telling her the whole story of your life.

4. Criticize

No one is saved from having a defect pair, and your appointment is no exception. Surely, you will notice a couple of things that you will not like at all when you start meeting your girl.

Nevertheless, what you should never do is criticize it directly on the first date. One because it is not characteristic of an educated man, and another because perhaps they are small defects that she can correct if later you let her know.

On a first date, you have to worry about having a good time, and then you can decide if you feel any interest in seeing her again.

5. Neglect your dress

Admittedly, for men, it does not apply too strict a protocol when dressing for a first date, but that does not mean that you must completely neglect yourself.

You must make a small effort to look attractive and seductive.

Choose your outfit according to where your date will be and try to look mature and sophisticated to leave it wanting you.

6. Don't be fun

This mistake is one of the most serious and is the one that decides if you will have a second date with your girl.

Making her have fun and spend a pleasant moment by your side should be your primary objective. You must make her laugh and show her with a smile on your lips that you are enjoying her company.

www.ingramcontent.com/pod-product-compliance
Lightning Source LLC
Chambersburg PA
CBHW070101120526
44589CB00033B/1345